Hot Topics

Flashcards For Passing the
PMP® and CAPM® Exams

Fifth Edition

S0-BIV-785

Rita Mulcahy, PMP

ISBN 1-932735-01-1
Library of Congress Control Number:
2005905459
Printed in the U.S.A.

For more information see:
E-mail: info@rmcproject.com
Web: www.rmcproject.com
Phone: 952.846.4484

WARNING: This is not a stand–alone product! You will need other review materials in order to pass the PMP or CAPM exam. We make no warranties or representations that use of these materials will result in passage of either exam. This book is designed to work with the book *PMP Exam Prep* 5th Edition by Rita Mulcahy, PMP, available at www.rmcproject.com. If you are studying for the PMP exam, use the chapter references on each Hot Topics flashcard to find further information in the PMP Exam Prep Book.

Table of Contents

How To Use This Book: This book has been updated for the *PMBOK® Guide - Third Edition*, designed as a portable reference to the Hot Topics on the PMP and CAPM exams, to be used to improve test taking speed and information recall. Note that the Professional and Social Responsibility chapter is not covered in the CAPM exam.

Read the front of each page and see if you can recall the items on the back of the page and know what they mean. If studying for the PMP exam, Hot Topics you are unfamiliar with should be reviewed in the book *PMP Exam Prep*, 5th Edition and the *PMBOK® Guide*. An audio version of Hot Topics is also available on CD-ROM.

About Us

- Rita Mulcahy, PMP, is an internationally recognized expert in project management and a sought after speaker, trainer and author. She has six project management books and products to her credit, and was a Contributor and Reviewer to the *PMBOK® Guide - Third Edition*.

- Rita has spoken at PMI's annual project management symposium to standing room only crowds and has been asked to present encores for an unheard of four years!

- RMC Project Management, Inc. provides Tricks of the Trade® for project management, PMP exam prep and advanced project management training.

See us at www.rmcproject.com.

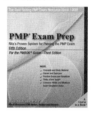

 **PM FASTrack® Exam Simulation Software**

Based on a psychometric review with more than 1,300 questions in six testing modes.

Take A Course:

Project Management Tricks of the Trade® – A three-day PM course covering the project management process using PMI terminology with real-world applications.

The PMP Exam Prep Course
This two-day accelerated learning course is designed to help you prepare for the PMP Exam with the most understanding of project management and the least amount of study! Study less than 40 hours after taking the course! This course includes the PMP Exam Prep System.

What is the definition of a project?

- Temporary

- Unique

- Progressively elaborated

See the Framework Chapter

What is the definition of a
program?

A group of interrelated projects, managed in a coordinated way

See the Framework Chapter

What is a product life cycle?

The cycle of a product's life from conception to withdrawal

See the Framework Chapter

What is a project life cycle?

What you need to do to
DO the work

It varies by industry and
type of project

See the Framework Chapter

What is the project
management process?

What you need to do to
MANAGE the work

- Initiating

- Planning

- Executing

- Monitoring and
  controlling

- Closing

See the Framework Chapter

What is a project
management office?

A department that centralizes the management of projects

The PMO provides templates and guidelines, shares lessons learned between projects and is represented on the change control board

See the Framework Chapter

What is a constraint?

Anything that limits the team's options

These include:

- Imposed milestone dates

- Cash flow requirements

- Resources available

See the Framework Chapter

What are the components
of the "triple constraint"?

What is it used for?

- Cost

- Time

- Scope

- Quality

- Risk

- Customer satisfaction

It is used to help evaluate
competing demands

See the Framework Chapter

Who are stakeholders?

Anyone whose interests may be positively or negatively impacted by the project, including:

- Project manager
- Customer
- Sponsor
- Performing organization
- Team
- Funding sources
- End user
- Society
- PMO

See the Framework Chapter

What should we do with stakeholders?

- Identify all stakeholders

- Determine all of their requirements

- Determine all of their expectations

- Communicate with them

- Manage their influence

See the Framework Chapter

What are three primary
forms of organization?

- Functional

- Projectized

- Matrix

See the Framework Chapter

What is a functional
organization?

The company is grouped by areas of specialization (e.g., accounting, marketing)

See the Framework Chapter

What is a projectized
organization?

The company is grouped by project

The team has no department to go to at project end

The project manager has total control of the resources

See the Framework Chapter

What is a matrix
organization?

A blend of functional and projectized organization where the team members have two bosses

See the Framework Chapter

What is a strong matrix
organization?

A matrix organization where the balance of power rests with the project manager instead of the functional manager

See the Framework Chapter

What is a weak matrix
organization?

A matrix organization where the balance of power rests with the functional manager instead of the project manager

Project management roles include:

- Project expediter

- Project coordinator

See the Framework Chapter

What is a balanced matrix organization?

An organization where power is equally balanced between project managers and functional managers

This is the preferred form of matrix

See the Framework Chapter

What is the process of
integration management?

- Develop project charter
- Develop preliminary project scope statement
- Develop project management plan
- Direct and manage project execution
- Monitor and control project work
- Integrated change control
- Close project

See the Integration Chapter

What are the methods to
select a project?

- Benefit measurement (comparative)

- Constrained optimization (mathematical)

See the Integration Chapter

What is develop project management plan?

What is its output?

The process of creating a project management plan that is bought into, approved, realistic and formal

Output: The project management plan

See the Integration Chapter

What is the preliminary
project scope statement?

Created with input from the sponsor, it is the first attempt to determine the project scope

What must be done to accomplish the project objectives

See the Integration Chapter

What are key outputs of
direct and manage project
execution?

- Deliverables

- Requested changes

- Implemented change
  requests, corrective
  and preventive actions
  and defect repair

See the Integration Chapter

What are key outputs of
monitor and control
project work?

- Recommended corrective actions, preventive actions and defect repair

- Requested changes

- Forecasts

See the Integration Chapter

What are key outputs of
integrated change control?

- Approved change requests, corrective actions, preventive actions and defect repair

- Rejected change requests

- Validated defect repair

- Deliverables

See the Integration Chapter

What are key outputs of close project?

- Administrative and contract closure procedures

- Final product

- Formal acceptance

- Project files

- Project closure documents

- Organizational process assets updates

See the Integration Chapter

Explain the project manager's role as integrator.

Making sure all the pieces of the project are properly coordinated and put together into one cohesive whole

See the Integration Chapter

What are baselines?

Parts of project management plan used to measure performance against

Includes:

- Schedule baseline
- Scope baseline
- Cost baseline
- Quality baseline
- Performance measurement baselines

Can change with approved changes

See the Integration Chapter

What is the project
statement of work?

Describes need, product scope and how project fits into the strategic plan

Created by the customer/sponsor prior to the beginning of the project

Is later refined into the preliminary and project scope statements

See the Integration Chapter

What is a work
authorization system?

A formal procedure for sanctioning project work to ensure work is done at the right time, and in the proper sequence

See the Integration Chapter

What is configuration management?

Making sure everyone knows what version of the scope, schedule and other components of the project management plan are the latest versions

See the Integration Chapter

What is a change control
system?

A system of formal procedures, set up in advance, defining how project deliverables and documentation are controlled, changed and approved

See the Integration Chapter

What are enterprise
environmental factors?

When are they used?

Company culture and existing systems that the project will have to deal with or can make use of

Used throughout the project management process

See the Integration Chapter

What are organizational
process assets?

When are they used?

- Company processes and procedures

- Historical information

- Lessons learned

Used throughout the project management process

See the Integration Chapter

What is historical information?

Records of past projects
used to plan and manage
future projects

Records of current project
to become part of
organizational process
assets

See the Integration Chapter

What is a project management information system?

The manual and automated system to submit and track changes, and monitor and control project activities

See the Integration Chapter

What is a change control
board?

Who may be on it?

A group of people that approves or rejects changes

May include:

- Project manager
- Customer
- Outside experts
- Sponsor
- Others

See the Integration Chapter

What are change requests?

When are they approved?

Formal requests to change
parts of the project after
the project management
plan is approved

They are approved in
integrated change control

See the Integration Chapter

What are preventive actions?

Actions taken to deal with anticipated or possible deviations from the performance baselines

See the Integration Chapter

What are corrective actions?

Actions taken to bring expected future project performance in line with the project management plan

See the Integration Chapter

What is a project charter?

How does it help the project?

A document issued by the sponsor during project initiating that:

- Formally recognizes the existence of the project
- Gives the project manager authority
- Documents the business need, justification, customer requirements and the product or service to satisfy those requirements

See the Scope Chapter

What is the process of
scope management?

- Scope planning

- Scope definition

- Create WBS

- Scope verification

- Scope control

See the Scope Chapter

What is the key output of
scope planning?

Project scope management plan

See the Scope Chapter

What are the key outputs
of scope definition?

- Project scope statement

- Requested changes

See the Scope Chapter

What are the key outputs of create WBS?

- Workbreakdown structure (WBS)

- WBS dictionary

- Scope baseline

- Requested changes

See the Scope Chapter

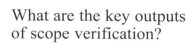

What are the key outputs
of scope verification?

- Customer formal acceptance of project deliverables

- Requested changes

See the Scope Chapter

What are the key outputs
of scope control?

- Accepted deliverables

- Requested changes

- Recommended corrective actions

See the Scope Chapter

What is the definition of
scope management?

- Doing all the work,
  and only the work,
  included in the project

- Determining if work is
  included in the project
  or not

See the Scope Chapter

What is a scope
management plan?

Part of the project
management plan

A plan for how scope will
be planned, executed and
controlled

See the Scope Chapter

What is a project scope
statement?

What are the key items
included?

A written description of
the project deliverables
and the work required to
create those deliverables

It includes:
- Project objectives
- Product scope
- Project requirements
- Project boundaries
- Project deliverables
- Product acceptance
  criteria
- Project constraints and
  assumptions

See the Scope Chapter

Stakeholder analysis is part
of which scope management
process?

Stakeholder analysis occurs during the process of scope definition.

See the Scope Chapter

Product analysis is
part of which scope
management process?

Product analysis occurs
during the process of
scope definition.

See the Scope Chapter

What is a work breakdown structure (WBS)?

What is it used for in planning?

Created during project planning by the team and used to define or decompose the project into smaller, more manageable pieces

Used to help determine project staffing, estimating, scheduling and risk management

See the Scope Chapter

What do work breakdown
structures show?

- Hierarchy

- Interrelationships

- Work packages

- Control account

- Numbering system

See the Scope Chapter

What is scope
decomposition?

Subdividing the major
deliverables into smaller,
more manageable
components

See the Scope Chapter

What is a WBS
dictionary?

A description of the work
to be done for each work
package

See the Scope Chapter

How are work packages
different from activities?

Activities are generated
from each work package

Work packages are shown
in a WBS

Activities are shown in an
activity list and network
diagram

See the Scope Chapter

What is scope
verification?

When is it done?

The process of formalizing acceptance of the project scope by the stakeholders/customer

It is done during project monitoring and controlling and at the end of each phase of the project life cycle

See the Scope Chapter

What is the difference
between product scope
and project scope?

Product scope is requirements

Project scope is the project management work needed to accomplish the product scope

See the Scope Chapter

What makes up the scope baseline?

- Scope statement

- WBS

- WBS dictionary

See the Scope Chapter

What is the process of
time management?

- Schedule management planning

- Activity definition

- Activity sequencing

- Activity resource estimating

- Activity duration estimating

- Schedule development

- Schedule control

See the Time Chapter

What is the key output of schedule management planning?

A schedule management
plan

See the Time Chapter

What is the key output of
activity definition?

See the Time Chapter

Activity list

What is the key output of activity sequencing?

Network diagram

See the Time Chapter

What is the key output of
activity resource
estimating?

Activity resource requirements

See the Time Chapter

What is the key output of
activity duration
estimating?

Activity duration estimates

See the Time Chapter

What is schedule development?

What are its key outputs?

The actions and tools necessary to create a bought into, approved, realistic and formal project schedule

Outputs:

- Project schedule

- Schedule baseline

- Requested changes

See the Time Chapter

What are key outputs of
schedule control?

- Schedule updates

- Performance measurements

- Recommended corrective actions

- Requested changes

See the Time Chapter

How is an AOA diagram different from a AON diagram?

An AOA diagram has only finish-to-start relationships

An AON diagram can have four relationships between activities

See the Time Chapter

What are mandatory
dependencies and
discretionary
dependencies?

<u>Mandatory</u>: One activity MUST be done after or before another
May also be called hard logic

<u>Discretionary</u>: When you PREFER activities to be accomplished in a certain order
May also be called:
- Preferred
- Preferential
- Soft logic

See the Time Chapter

What are external
dependencies?

Based on the needs of a party OUTSIDE the project

See the Time Chapter

What is a resource
breakdown structure?

A hierarchical list of identified resources by category

See the Time Chapter

What is a schedule model?

Why is it used?

A tool to perform schedule network analysis

See the Time Chapter

What is the critical path?

How does it help the
project?

The longest path in the network diagram that tells you the shortest time in which the project can be completed

Tells the project manager where to focus his time

Helps to shorten the length of the project

See the Time Chapter

What is the near-critical
path?

The path closest in length
to the critical path

See the Time Chapter

Define lag.

Waiting time inserted into the schedule

See the Time Chapter

Define total float and the
formula for total float.

The amount of time an activity can be delayed without delaying the project

Formula:

Late start – Early start
OR
Late finish – Early finish

See the Time Chapter

Define free float and
project float.

<u>Free Float</u>: The amount of time an activity can be delayed without delaying the early start date of its successor

<u>Project Float</u>: The amount of time the project can be delayed without affecting a project's required due date

The desired project end date less the actual end date.

See the Time Chapter

What are the methods to
compress a schedule?

- Crashing

- Fast tracking

- Re-estimating

See the Time Chapter

What is crashing?

Schedule compression through analyzing cost and schedule trade-offs to obtain the greatest compression for the least cost while maintaining scope

See the Time Chapter

What is fast tracking?

Schedule compression by doing more critical path activities in parallel

See the Time Chapter

What is the critical chain
method?

A schedule network
analysis tool that makes
use of buffers

See the Time Chapter

What is re-estimating?

Decreasing project and/or activity cost by eliminating the risks in activities

See the Time Chapter

What is resource leveling?

Keeping the amount of resources used for each time period constant, thus affecting the project duration

See the Time Chapter

What is a schedule
management plan?

Part of the project
management plan

A plan for how the
schedule will be planned,
executed and controlled

See the Time Chapter

What is the schedule baseline?

Approved schedule with any approved changes, used to measure project schedule performance

See the Time Chapter

What are the main tools
for displaying a schedule?

- Network diagrams

- Bar charts

- Milestone charts

- Flowcharts

See the Time Chapter

What do network
diagrams show?

- Interdependencies between activities

- How project activities will flow from beginning to end

- When estimates are added

- May also be used to find the critical path

See the Time Chapter

What do simple bar charts show?

Project schedule or project status

See the Time Chapter

What do milestone charts
show?

High-level project status

See the Time Chapter

What do flowcharts show?

Work flow or process flow through a system

See the Time Chapter

What is a Monte Carlo analysis?

A schedule network analysis technique

Used to simulate the project to determine how likely you are to get the project completed by any specific date or for any specific cost

Also used in quantitative risk analysis to determine an overall level of risk on the project

See the Time Chapter

What are the following rules?

50/50 rule

20/80 rule

0/100 rule

Methods of progress reporting

50 percent of the effort is reported complete (20 percent or 0 percent) when an activity begins

The balance (50 percent, 80 percent or 100 percent) is recorded only when an activity is finished

See the Time Chapter

What is the process of cost management?

- Cost management planning

- Cost estimating

- Cost budgeting

- Cost control

See the Cost Chapter

What is a key output of cost management planning?

Cost management plan

See the Cost Chapter

What are key outputs of
cost estimating?

- Activity cost estimates

- Requested changes

See the Cost Chapter

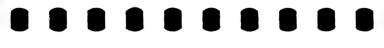

What are key outputs of cost budgeting?

- Cost baseline

- Funding requirements

- Requested changes

See the Cost Chapter

What are key outputs of
cost control?

- Requested changes

- Performance measurements

- Recommended corrective actions

- Forecasted completion

See the Cost Chapter

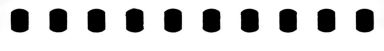

Name some inputs to
estimating.

- Project scope statement
- Work breakdown structure
- Network diagram
- Schedule and management plan
- Enterprise environmental factors
- Organizational process assets
- Resource pool
- Project management effort
- Risk management plan and register
- Project objectives

See the Cost Chapter

What is a cost
management plan?

Part of the project
management plan

How cost will be planned,
executed and controlled

See the Cost Chapter

What are the main
approaches to cost or
schedule estimating?

- Analogous estimating

- Bottom-up estimating (cost only)

- Parametric estimating

- Three-point estimates

- One-time estimates

See the Cost Chapter

What is analogous
estimating?

Top-down estimating that looks at the past to predict the future

"The last three projects cost $25,000, or took six months, and so should this one"

See the Cost Chapter

What is bottom-up
estimating?

Estimating based on the details of the project, e.g., from the bottom of the work breakdown structure

See the Cost Chapter

What is parametric
estimating?

Extrapolating from historical information to estimate costs, e.g., cost per line of code, hours per installation

See the Cost Chapter

What is earned value
analysis?

A method of measuring project performance that looks at the value earned for work accomplished

Can be used to predict future cost performance and project completion dates

See the Cost Chapter

What is the range for an
order of magnitude
estimate?

-50 percent to +100
percent from actual

See the Cost Chapter

What is the difference
between a cost budget and
a cost baseline?

Cost budget adds
management reserve to
the cost baseline

See the Cost Chapter

What is the formula for
cost variance?

$$EV - AC = CV$$

See the Cost Chapter

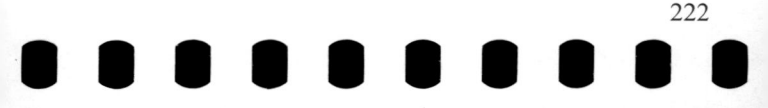

What is the formula for
schedule variance?

See the Cost Chapter

$$EV - PV = SV$$

What is the formula for
cost performance index?

See the Cost Chapter

$$EV / AC = CPI$$

What is the formula for
schedule performance
index?

$$EV / PV = SPI$$

See the Cost Chapter

What are the formulas for
estimate at completion?

- BAC / CPI = EAC

  or

- AC + ETC

- AC + BAC - EV

- $\dfrac{AC + (BAC - EV)}{CPI}$

See the Cost Chapter

What is the formula for
estimate to complete?

$$EAC - AC = ETC$$

See the Cost Chapter

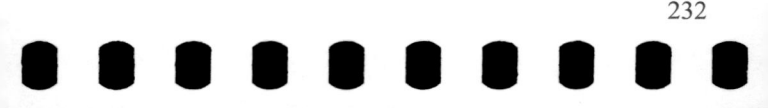

What is the formula for
variance at completion?

$$BAC - EAC = VAC$$

See the Cost Chapter

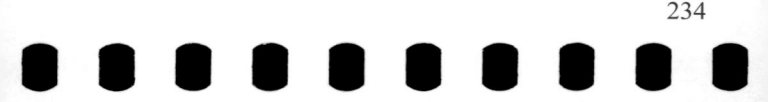

Define present value.

The value today of future cash flows

$$PV = \frac{FV}{(1 + r)^n}$$

See the Cost Chapter

Define net present value.

The value in today's
dollars of some future
costs and expenses

For cost, the lower the
number the better

For revenue, the higher the
number the better

See the Cost Chapter

Define internal rate of return.

The rate an investment in
the project will return

The higher the number the
better

The rate at which a
project's inflows and
outflows are equal

See the Cost Chapter

Define payback period.

The number of time
periods to recover the
investment

A lower number is better
than a higher one

See the Cost Chapter

Define benefit cost ratio.

$$\frac{\text{Benefit}}{\text{Cost}}$$

The higher the number the better

See the Cost Chapter

Define opportunity cost.

The opportunity given up
by selecting one project
over another

See the Cost Chapter

What are sunk costs?

Expended costs

See the Cost Chapter

Define the law of
diminishing returns.

The more you put into the
effort, the less you get out
of it

See the Cost Chapter

Define working capital.

Current assets minus
current liabilities

The amount of funds
available to spend on
projects

See the Cost Chapter

Describe a variable cost
and a fixed cost
chargeable to the project.

<u>Variable Cost</u>: A cost that varies with the amount of work done on the project

<u>Fixed Cost</u>: A cost that does not vary with the amount of work done on the project

See the Cost Chapter

Describe a direct cost and
an indirect cost chargeable
to the project.

<u>Direct Cost</u>: A cost directly attributable to the project

<u>Indirect Cost</u>: Overhead

See the Cost Chapter

What are different types of depreciation?

<u>Straight Line Depreciation</u>: Depreciate same amount each time period

<u>Accelerated Depreciation</u>: Depreciate an amount greater than straight line each time period

See the Cost Chapter

What does life cycle
costing mean?

Considering the future cost of operating and maintaining the project or deliverable over its life when planning and managing the project

See the Cost Chapter

What is value analysis?

Finding a less costly way
of doing essentially the
same work

See the Cost Chapter

What is the process of
quality management?

- Quality planning

- Quality assurance

- Quality control

See the Quality Chapter

What are key outputs of
quality planning?

- Quality management plan

- Quality metrics

- Quality baseline

- Process improvement plan

See the Quality Chapter

What are key outputs of
perform quality assurance?

See the Quality Chapter

- **Requested changes**

- **Recommended corrective actions**

What are key outputs of
perform quality control?

- Quality control measurements

- Validated defect repair

- Requested changes

- Recommended corrective and preventive actions and defect repair

See the Quality Chapter

What does gold plating
mean?

Adding extra items and services that do not necessarily contribute added value or quality to customer deliverables

See the Quality Chapter

What is marginal analysis?

An analysis to determine when optimal quality is reached

An analysis to determine the point where incremental revenue from improvement equals the incremental cost to secure it

See the Quality Chapter

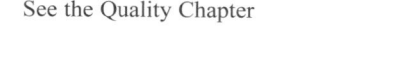

What is a quality
management plan?

Part of the project
management plan

A plan for how the project
management team will
implement the performing
organization's quality
policy

See the Quality Chapter

What is a process
improvement plan?

A plan for analyzing processes used on the project to decrease defects, save time and money and increase customer satisfaction

See the Quality Chapter

What is the quality
baseline?

What is it used for?

The project's quality
objectives

One of the baselines used
to measure performance
against

See the Quality Chapter

What are quality metrics?

Specific measures of quality to be used on the project in quality assurance and quality control

See the Quality Chapter

What does continuous
improvement mean?

The never-ending enhancement of a product/service through small, continuous enhancements

See the Quality Chapter

How much inventory is maintained in a just in time environment?

How does this affect attention to quality?

Little inventory is
maintained

It forces attention to
quality

See the Quality Chapter

What does ISO 9000
stand for?

One of the *International Organization for Standardization* (ISO) international quality standards that asks, "Do you have a quality standard, and are you following it?"

See the Quality Chapter

What is the definition of
total quality management?

A comprehensive management philosophy of encouraging the finding of ways to continuously improve the quality of business practices, products or services

See the Quality Chapter

What does the phrase
prevention over inspection
mean?

The cost of avoiding or preventing mistakes is always much less than the cost of correcting them

See the Quality Chapter

What does mutually
exclusive mean?

Two events that cannot
occur in a single trial

For example, you can't
roll a 5 and a 6 on one die

See the Quality Chapter

What does statistical
independence mean?

The probability of "B" occurring does not depend on "A" occurring

For example, the outcome of a second dice roll is not influenced by (dependent on) the outcome of the first roll

See the Quality Chapter

What is a normal
distribution curve?

Symmetric bell-shaped
frequency distribution
curve

The most common
probability distribution

See the Quality Chapter

What do three sigma and
six sigma refer to?

Often used as quality standards.

<u>Three Sigma</u>: +/- Three standard deviations from the distribution mean under which 99.73% of all items are acceptable

<u>Six Sigma</u>: +/- Six standard deviations from the mean under which 99.999998% of all items are acceptable
A higher quality standard than three sigma

See the Quality Chapter

What is the difference
between a population and
a sample?

<u>Population</u>: The total number of individual members, items or elements comprising a uniquely defined group

For example: All women

<u>Sample</u>: A subset of population members

For example: Women over the age of 30 in England

See the Quality Chapter

Who has responsibility for
quality on a project?

The project manager is ultimately responsible, but the team members must inspect their own work

See the Quality Chapter

What are the impacts of
poor quality?

- Higher costs

- Increased rework

- Lower morale

- Lower customer satisfaction

- Increased risk

See the Quality Chapter

Name costs of conformance and costs of nonconformance.

Which costs should be greater?

What does cost of nonconformance mean?

Provide examples.

<u>Costs of conformance</u>:
- Quality training
- Studies
- Surveys

The costs of conformance should be less than the costs of nonconformance.

<u>Costs of nonconformance</u>:
- Rework
- Scrap
- Inventory costs
- Warranty costs

Costs of nonconformance are associated with poor quality.

See the Quality Chapter

What is the purpose of
quality planning?

- Find existing quality standards and processes
- Create additional project specific processes and standards
- Determine what work you will do to meet those standards
- Determine how you will measure
- Create quality plan

See the Quality Chapter

Name some of the tools
used in quality planning.

- Benchmarking

- Cost-benefit analysis

- Design of experiments

- Cost of quality

See the Quality Chapter

Define benchmarking.

Comparing your company
or department's
performance to those of
other companies

See the Quality Chapter

Define cost-benefit
analysis.

Comparing the costs of an effort to the benefits of that effort

See the Quality Chapter

What is a design of
experiments?

A statistical method for changing important variables to determine what combination will improve overall quality

See the Quality Chapter

What is the purpose of
quality assurance?

- Making sure all processes are used on the project and performing continuous process improvement
- Determine if activities comply with processes
- Continuous improvement
- Identify improvements the company needs to make
- Recommend changes

See the Quality Chapter

What are some of the
activities in quality
assurance?

- Process analysis

- Quality audits

See the Quality Chapter

What are quality audits?

Structured reviews of quality activities that identify lessons learned

See the Quality Chapter

What is the purpose of
quality control?

- Measure specific project results against quality standards
- Make changes to quality baseline
- Identify root causes and quality improvements
- Recommend corrective and preventive actions, changes, and defect repair
- Validate deliverables

See the Quality Chapter

Name the quality control tools.

- Cause and effect diagram

- Flowchart

- Histogram

- Pareto chart

- Run chart

- Scatter diagram

- Control chart

See the Quality Chapter

What is defect repair?

Rework when a component of the project does not meet specifications

Discovered during quality control, formed into change requests during monitor and control project work, and approved or rejected during integrated change control

See the Quality Chapter

What is a cause and effect (fishbone) diagram?

Why is it used?

Creative way to look at
the causes or potential
causes of a problem

Used to explore the future
or the past

Also called a fishbone or
Ishikawa diagram

Maybe used in quality
planning or control

See the Quality Chapter

What is a checklist?

A list of items to inspect
or a picture of an item that
is marked to show
locations of defects found
during inspection

See the Quality Chapter

What does a Pareto chart show?

Why is it used?

Graphically prioritizes causes of process problems (by frequency of occurrence) to help focus attention on the most critical issues affecting quality

See the Quality Chapter

What is the 80/20 rule?

80 percent of process problems are caused by 20 percent of the causes

See the Quality Chapter

What is statistical sampling?

Inspecting by choosing
only part of a population
(a sample) to test

See the Quality Chapter

What is a control chart?

Specialized trend chart documenting whether a measured process is in or out of statistical control

See the Quality Chapter

What are control limits?

The acceptable range of variation on a control chart

See the Quality Chapter

What are the specification
limits on a control chart?

Customer's measures
defining acceptable
product/service
characteristics and
tolerances

See the Quality Chapter

What does out of control mean?

The process is performing neither consistently nor predictably, due to the existence of assignable causes

See the Quality Chapter

What does the rule of
seven mean?

Seven consecutive data points appearing on a control chart on one side of the mean, suggesting that the process is out of statistical control

See the Quality Chapter

What is a special cause?

A data point on a control chart or rule of seven indicating that the measured process is out of statistical control and that the cause(s) of the event must be investigated

See the Quality Chapter

What is the process of
human resource
management?

- Human resource planning

- Acquire project team

- Develop project team

- Manage project team

See the Human Resources Chapter

What are key outputs of
human resource planning?

- Roles and responsibilities

- Staffing management plan

- Project organizational chart

See the Human Resources Chapter

What are key outputs of
acquire project team?

- Project staff (team) assignment

- Resource availability

See the Human Resources Chapter

What is a key output of
develop project team?

Team performance assessment: Evaluating team effectiveness

See the Human Resources Chapter

What are key outputs of
manage project team?

- **Requested changes**

- **Recommended preventive and corrective actions**

See the Human Resources Chapter

Describe the roles and responsibilities of all the people involved in a project.

This topic cannot be summarized here, but it is critical to understand who does what on the exam.

See the Human Resources Chapter in PMP Exam Prep for more on this topic.

See the Human Resources Chapter

Define sponsor.

- Provides information for preliminary project scope statement

- Issues the charter

- Provides funding

- May dictate dates

- Approves project management plan

- Agrees to the change control board

- Is involved in risk

See the Human Resources Chapter

Describe the team's role.

- Create the work breakdown structure and help with project management planning

- Estimate activities

- Complete activities

- Help control and close out the project

- Held accountable for assigned activities

See the Human Resources Chapter

Define the role of the
stakeholders.

They may help:

- Plan the project

- Approve changes

- Identify constraints

- Perform the risk management process

See the Human Resources Chapter

Define the role of
functional managers.

Resource managers:

- Participate in planning
- Approve final project management plan
- Approve final schedule
- Assist with problems related to team member performance

See the Human Resources Chapter

What are the key elements in a staffing management plan?

When and how human resource requirements will be met

- Recognition and rewards
- Staff acquisition
- Timetable
- Release criteria
- Training needs

See the Human Resources Chapter

What must a project manager do in order to develop the project team?

- Hold team building activities throughout the project life

- Obtain and provide training where needed

- Establish ground rules

- Create and give recognition and rewards

- Place team members in the same location (co-location)

See the Human Resources Chapter

What must a project manager do to manage a project team?

- Observe
- Use an issue log
- Keep in touch
- Complete project performance appraisals
- Actively look for and help resolve conflicts that the team cannot resolve on their own

See the Human Resources Chapter

What is a team
performance assessment?

An assessment by the project manager of project team effectiveness

See the Human Resources Chapter

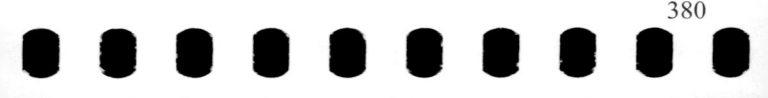

Name the powers of the
project manager.

- Formal

- Reward

- Penalty

- Expert

- Referent

See the Human Resources Chapter

Name the different
leadership styles a project
manager may choose to
use.

- Directing

- Facilitating

- Coaching

- Supportive

- Autocratic

- Consultative

- Consensus

See the Human Resources Chapter

Name the most common
sources of conflict on
projects.

- Schedules

- Priorities

- Resources

- Technical opinions

NOT personalities

See the Human Resources Chapter

Name conflict resolution
techniques.

- Problem solving
  (confronting)

- Compromise

- Withdrawal
  (avoidance)

- Smoothing

- Forcing

See the Human Resources Chapter

Define problem solving.

Define compromising.

<u>Problem Solving</u>: Solving
the real problem
(Win-win)

<u>Compromising</u>: Making
all parties somewhat
happy
(Lose-lose)

See the Human Resources Chapter

390

Define withdrawal.

Define smoothing.

Define forcing.

<u>Withdrawal</u>: Postponing a project decision or avoiding addressing the problem

<u>Smoothing</u>: Emphasizing agreement rather than differences of opinion

<u>Forcing</u>: Do it my way

See the Human Resources Chapter

What are the project
manager's human resource
responsibilities?

- Create a team directory
- Negotiate for best resources
- Create project-related job descriptions for team members
- Make sure team members obtain needed training
- Create reward systems
- Create a staffing management plan

See the Human Resources Chapter

What is a project
performance appraisal?

An evaluation of
individual team member
effectiveness

See the Human Resources Chapter

What is Maslow's theory?

People are motivated
according to hierarchy:

- Self-actualization

- Esteem

- Social

- Safety

- Physiological

See the Human Resources Chapter

What did McGregor
describe?

<u>Theory X</u>: Managers who accept this theory believe that people need to be watched every second

<u>Theory Y</u>: Managers who accept this theory believe that people want to achieve and can work without supervision

See the Human Resources Chapter

What did Herzberg
describe?

See the Human Resources Chapter

- Hygiene factors

- Motivating agents

Why is releasing resources
the last activity in closure?

The team and other resources are needed to complete closure

See the Communications Chapter

What is a kickoff meeting?

When does it occur?

A meeting of all parties to the project (project stakeholders, sellers, etc.) to make sure everyone is "on the same page"

It is held at the end of the planning process group.

See the Communications Chapter

What is the process of
communications
management?

- Communications planning

- Information distribution

- Performance reporting

- Manage stakeholders

See the Communications Chapter

What is the key output of
communications planning?

Communications
management plan

See the Communications Chapter

What are key outputs of
information distribution?

- Team and stakeholders have the information they need

- Requested changes

See the Communications Chapter

What are key outputs of
performance reporting?

- Stakeholders know how the project is performing

- Performance reports

- Forecasts

- Requested changes

- Recommended corrective actions

See the Communications Chapter

What are key outputs of
manage stakeholders?

- Resolved issues

- Approved change requests

- Approved corrective actions

See the Communications Chapter

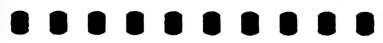

Define communications
planning.

Determining the information and communication needs of stakeholders

See the Communications Chapter

What is a communications
management plan?

Part of the project
management plan

A formal plan that
describes what will be
communicated and
received from whom,
when, and how often

See the Communications Chapter

Describe the information
distribution requirements
on projects.

Implementing the communications management plan

Creating reports including:

- Lessons learned
- Performance reports

See the Communications Chapter in PMP Exam Prep for more on this topic.

See the Communications Chapter

Describe the
communications model
and its components.

Messages are encoded, transmitted and unencoded, and must include attention to:

- Nonverbal communication
- Paralingual
- Active listening
- Effective listening
- Feedback

See the Communications Chapter

How much of
communication is
nonverbal?

About 55 percent

See the Communications Chapter

What does paralingual
mean?

Pitch and tone of voice

See the Communications Chapter

Name communications
methods.

- Formal

- Informal

- Written

- Verbal

See the Communications Chapter

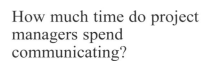

How much time do project managers spend communicating?

90 percent

See the Communications Chapter

Name communication
blockers.

- Noise

- Distance

- Improper encoding

- "That was a bad idea"

- Hostility

- Language

- Culture

See the Communications Chapter

Describe the rules for
effective meetings.

- Set a time limit
- Schedule in advance
- Create an agenda with team input
- Distribute agenda in advance
- Lead meeting with a set of rules

See the Communications Chapter in PMP Exam Prep for more on this topic.

See the Communications Chapter

What is the formula for
communication channels?

$$[N (N-1)] / 2$$

See the Communications Chapter

What is an issue log?

Documents project issues,
persons responsible for
resolving issues and target
resolution dates

See the Communications Chapter

What are lessons learned?

What do we do with
them?

What went right, wrong,
and could be done
differently

Used in planning a project
and are generated by the
project to be used by other
projects in the future

See the Communications Chapter

What is the process of risk management?

- Risk management planning

- Risk identification

- Qualitative risk analysis

- Quantitative risk analysis

- Risk response planning

- Risk monitoring and control

See the Risk Chapter

444

What is the key output of
risk management
planning?

Risk management plan

See the Risk Chapter

What are key outputs of
risk identification?

- Risks

- Risk register

See the Risk Chapter

What are key outputs of
qualitative risk analysis
added to the risk register?

- List of risks

- Ranked risks by category

- Watchlist

See the Risk Chapter

What are key outputs of
quantitative risk analysis
added to the risk register?

- Probability of achieving the cost and time objectives

- Prioritized list of quantified risks

See the Risk Chapter

What are key outputs of
risk response planning?

- Risk response plans
- Contingency plans
- Triggers
- Reserves for time and cost
- Fallback plans
- Contracts
- Revised project management plan
- Residual risks
- Secondary risks

See the Risk Chapter

What are key outputs of
risk monitoring and
control?

- Requested changes

- Recommended preventive and corrective actions

- Updates to the risk register

- Risk audits

- Periodic risk reviews

- Risks closed

See the Risk Chapter

Define risks.

Events that can affect a
project for better or worse

Threats and opportunities

See the Risk Chapter

Describe key things one needs to know about each risk.

- Probability

- Impact

- Timing

- Frequency

See the Risk Chapter

Someone who is risk averse is:

Unwilling to take risks

See the Risk Chapter

What is risk tolerance?

Amount of risk acceptable

See the Risk Chapter

Name the inputs to the
risk management process.

- Organizational process assets
- Enterprise environmental factors
- Project charter
- Project scope statement
- Project scope management plan
- Staffing plans
- WBS
- Network diagram
- Cost and time estimates

See the Risk Chapter

What are risk categories?

Lists of common sources of risk, including:

- Technical

- Project management

- Schedule

- Cost

- Others

See the Risk Chapter

What are risk
identification techniques?

- Documentation reviews
- Brainstorming
- Delphi Technique
- Root cause identification
- Interviewing
- SWOT
- Checklists
- Assumptions analysis
- Diagramming techniques

See the Risk Chapter

What are the types of risks?

- Business

- Pure

See the Risk Chapter

What are risk triggers?

Early warning signs that a
risk event is about to
occur

See the Risk Chapter

What is assumptions
analysis?

When is it done?

Explores the validity of
project assumptions to
identify new risks in risk
identification

See the Risk Chapter

What is risk data quality assessment?

When is it done?

- Reviewing how well understood is the risk

- A method to test reliability of risk information collected

- It is done during qualitative risk analysis

See the Risk Chapter

What is a probability and impact matrix?

The company's scale to determine which risks continue through the risk management process

See the Risk Chapter

What is the formula for
expected monetary value?

Probability times impact

See the Risk Chapter

What is a decision tree?

A model of a decision to be made which includes the probabilities and impacts of future events to help make a decision today

See the Risk Chapter

Who is a risk response
owner?

The person assigned to execute risk responses for each critical risk

See the Risk Chapter

Name and define the risk
response strategies for
threats.

<u>Avoid</u>: Eliminate a specific threat by eliminating the cause

<u>Mitigate</u>: Reduce the probability or impact

<u>Accept</u>:
Passive – Do nothing
If it happens, it happens.

Active – Develop contingency plans

<u>Transfer</u>: Make another party responsible for a risk

May include: outsourcing, insurance, warranties, bonds and guarantees

See the Risk Chapter

Name and define the risk response strategies for opportunities.

<u>Exploit</u>: Enhance the opportunity

<u>Share</u>: Allocate ownership to a third party

<u>Enhance</u>: Increase probability or impacts

<u>Accept</u>:
Passive – Do nothing
If it happens, it happens

Active – Develop contingency plans

See the Risk Chapter

What are residual risks?

Risks that remain after risk response planning:

- Risks for which contingency and fallback plans have been created

- Risks which have been accepted

Outputs of risk response planning

See the Risk Chapter

What are secondary risks?

New risks created by risk response strategies

Outputs of risk response planning

See the Risk Chapter

How does buying
insurance relate to risk
response planning?

It exchanges an unknown
risk for a known risk

It is a method to decrease
project risk

It is an output of risk
response planning

See the Risk Chapter

What do contracts have to
do with risk response
planning?

A contract helps allocate
and mitigate risks

A risk analysis is done
before a contract is signed

Contracts are outputs of
risk response planning

See the Risk Chapter

What are contingency
plans?

Planned responses to risks

Outputs of risk response
planning

See the Risk Chapter

What are fallback plans?

Actions that will be taken
if the contingency plan is
not effective

Outputs of risk response
planning

See the Risk Chapter

What does a revised
project management plan
have to do with risk
management?

The components of the project management plan will need to be updated based on the results of risk planning

It is an output of risk response planning

See the Risk Chapter

What are reserves?

Time or cost added to the project to account for risk

Also referred to as:

- Management reserve
- Contingency reserve

Reserves are outputs of risk response planning

See the Risk Chapter

What is a contingency
reserve?

Time or cost allocated to
cover known unknowns

Included in cost baseline

See the Risk Chapter

What is a management
reserve?

Time or cost allocated to
cover unknown unknowns

Included in cost budget

See the Risk Chapter

What are risk
reassessments?

When do they occur?

Identification of new risks

They occur during risk monitoring and control

See the Risk Chapter

What is reserve analysis?

When is it done?

- Determining reserves

- Managing the reserves and making sure the amount remaining is adequate

It is done during risk response planning, monitoring and controlling, activity duration estimating, cost budgeting and cost control

See the Risk Chapter

What are risk response
audits?

Examining and
documenting the
effectiveness of the risk
response and the risk
response owner

See the Risk Chapter

What is the process of
procurement management?

- Plan purchases and acquisitions

- Plan contracting

- Request seller responses

- Select sellers

- Contract administration

- Contract closure

See the Procurement Chapter

Name the inputs to the procurement management process.

- Enterprise environmental factors
- Organizational process assets
- WBS
- Risk register
- Project scope statement
- Project schedule
- Cost estimate for contracted work
- Cost baseline for the project

See the Procurement Chapter

What are key outputs of plan purchases and acquisitions?

- Procurement management plan

- Contract statement of work

- Requested changes

See the Procurement Chapter

What are key outputs of
plan contracting?

- Procurement documents

- Evaluation criteria

See the Procurement Chapter

What are key outputs of
request seller responses?

- Procurement
  documents

- Proposals

See the Procurement Chapter

What are key outputs of
select sellers?

- Contract signed

- Contract management
  plan

- Requested changes

See the Procurement Chapter

What are key outputs of
contract administration?

- Substantial completion

- Requested changes

- Recommended corrective actions

See the Procurement Chapter

What are key outputs of
contract closure?

- Product verification

- Financial closure

- Update and index records

- Performance reporting

- Procurement audits

- Lessons learned

- Formal acceptance

See the Procurement Chapter

What is a contract
management plan?

A plan for how each contract will be administered

See the Procurement Chapter

What is a procurement management plan?

Part of the project
management plan

Describes how
procurements will be
planned, executed and
controlled

See the Procurement Chapter

536

What is required for a
legal contract?

- Offer

- Acceptance

- Consideration

- Legal capacity

- Legal purpose

See the Procurement Chapter

What is a contract?

May include all of the following:

- Legal terms

- Business terms

- Contract statement of work

- Marketing literature

- Drawings

See the Procurement Chapter

Describe the project
manager's role in
procurement.

- Understand the procurement process
- Make sure the work described in the contract is complete
- Be involved in the whole contracting process
- Help tailor the contract to the project
- Incorporate mitigation and allocation of risks into the contract

See the Procurement Chapter

Name the advantages of
centralized contracting.

- Increased expertise in contracting

- Standardized practices

- Clear career path

See the Procurement Chapter

Name the disadvantages of
centralized contracting.

- One person works on many projects

- May be difficult to obtain contracting help when needed

See the Procurement Chapter

Name the advantages of
decentralized contracting.

- Easier access to contracting expertise

- More loyalty to the project

- More focused contract experience

See the Procurement Chapter

Name the disadvantages of
decentralized contracting.

- No home for the contracts person after the project

- Less focus on improving contracting expertise

- Inefficient use of resources

- Little standardization of contracting processes from one project to the next

See the Procurement Chapter

What does make-or-buy
refer to?

Analyzing whether the performing organization should do the work or buy the services/supplies from outside the organization

See the Procurement Chapter

What are the main types
of contracts?

- Cost reimbursable

- Fixed price

- Time and material

- Purchase order

See the Procurement Chapter

What is a cost
reimbursable contract?

All costs are reimbursed

See the Procurement Chapter

What is a cost plus fixed
fee contract?

All costs are reimbursed

The fee is fixed at a
certain monetary amount

See the Procurement Chapter

What is a cost plus
percentage of cost
contract?

All costs are reimbursed,
plus a specific percentage
of costs as fee or profit

See the Procurement Chapter

What is a cost plus
incentive fee contract?

Costs are reimbursed plus an incentive, usually an additional fee, for exceeding performance criteria that have been determined in advance

See the Procurement Chapter

What is a time and
material contract?

Usually a fixed hourly rate or a fixed cost per item, plus a reimbursable component for expenses or materials

See the Procurement Chapter

What is a fixed price
contract?

There is only one fee for accomplishing all the work

See the Procurement Chapter

What is a fixed price plus
incentive fee contract?

Total price is fixed, but an additional amount may be paid for exceeding performance criteria determined in advance

See the Procurement Chapter

What is a fixed price
economic price adjustment
contract?

A fixed price contract with an allowable adjustment for price increase, due to cost increases in later time periods

See the Procurement Chapter

Describe how contract administration efforts will be different with each contract form.

This critical concept
cannot be summarized
here.

*See the Procurement
Chapter in PMP Exam Prep
for more on this topic.*

See the Procurement Chapter

What is a purchase order?

A unilateral contract

See the Procurement Chapter

What are incentives?

What might they be used for?

Help bring the seller's objectives in line with the buyer's

Incentives for:

- Time

- Cost

- Quality

- Scope

See the Procurement Chapter

Who has the cost risk in a cost reimbursable contract?

In a fixed price contract?

Risk in a cost reimbursable contract is borne by the buyer

Risk in a fixed price contract is borne by the seller

See the Procurement Chapter

Name the types of contract
statements of work.

- Performance

- Functional/detailed

- Design

See the Procurement Chapter

What are procurement
documents?

- Request for proposal
  (RFP)

- Invitation for bid
  (IFB)

- Request for quotation
  (RFQ)

See the Procurement Chapter

What are standard contract
terms and conditions?

What are special
provisions?

<u>Standard Contract Terms and Provisions</u>: Terms and conditions which are used for all contracts within the company

<u>Special Provisions</u>: Terms and conditions created for the unique needs of the project

Created with the input of the project manager

See the Procurement Chapter

Name common terms and
conditions that may be in
a contract.

Please review the long list of terms and conditions and what they mean in PMP Exam Prep, Procurement Chapter.

See the Procurement Chapter

What is a letter of intent?

A letter from the buyer,
without legal binding,
saying the buyer intends to
hire the seller

See the Procurement Chapter

What does privity refer to?

Contractual relationships between two or more companies

See the Procurement Chapter

What does non-competitive
procurement mean?

Work awarded to a single source or sole source without competition

See the Procurement Chapter

When are evaluation
criteria created and used?

What do they refer to?

Created during plan
contracting

Rationale that the buyer
will use to weight or score
suppliers' proposals

Used during select sellers
to pick a supplier

See the Procurement Chapter

What is a bidder
conference?

What should be watched
out for?

A meeting with prospective sellers to make sure all understand the procurement and have a chance to ask questions

Watch for:

- Collusion

- Sellers not asking questions

- All questions and answers are distributed to all

See the Procurement Chapter

What is a qualified
seller list?

A list of sellers who have
been pre-approved

See the Procurement Chapter

What are the objectives of
negotiation?

- Obtain a fair and reasonable price

- Develop a good relationship with the other side

See the Procurement Chapter

Name some negotiation
tactics.

- Attacks
- Personal insults
- Good guy/Bad guy
- Deadline
- Lying
- Limited authority
- Missing man
- Delay
- Extreme demands
- Withdrawal
- Fait accompli

See the Procurement Chapter

Name some of the project manager's activities during contract administration.

- Review invoices
- Integrated change control
- Interpret the contract
- Monitor performance against the contract
- Risk management

Please see the long list in PMP Exam Prep, Procurement Chapter.

See the Procurement Chapter

Why might there be
conflict between the
contract administrator and
the project manager?

The contract administrator is the only one with the power to change the contract (including the project scope)

See the Procurement Chapter

What is a contract change
control system?

A system created to modify the contract and to control changes to the contract

See the Procurement Chapter

What must be done for all
contract changes?

They must be formally
documented

See the Procurement Chapter

What is the purpose of a
buyer-conducted
performance review?

Identify seller's successes or failures, and allow the buyer to rate the seller's ability to perform

See the Procurement Chapter

Define claims
administration.

Managing contested
changes and constructive
changes (claims) requested
by the seller

See the Procurement Chapter

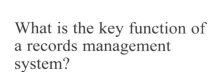

What is the key function of
a records management
system?

Maintain an index of
contract documentation
and records to assist in
retrieval

Part of the project
management information
system

See the Procurement Chapter

Name the guidelines for
interpreting what is or is
not included in the
contract.

617

*See the Procurement
Chapter in PMP Exam Prep
for more on this topic.*

See the Procurement Chapter

What is the purpose of contract closure in the procurement management process?

- Perform a procurement audit

- Complete the work done under contract

See the Procurement Chapter

What is a procurement audit?

Structured review of the procurement process and determination of lessons learned to help other procurements

See the Procurement Chapter

What does professional
and social responsibility
mean?

- Ensure individual integrity
- Contribute to the project management knowledge base
- Enhance personal professional competence
- Promote interaction among stakeholders

For the PMP exam, make sure you read the extensive information on this topic in PMP Exam Prep, Prof. Responsibility Chapter.

See the Prof. Responsibility Chapter

What does "ensure
individual integrity" mean?

- Follow PMI's code of professional conduct
- Tell the truth in reports
- Follow copyright and other laws
- Treat others with respect
- Report violations
- Do not put personal gain over project needs
- Do not give or take bribes

See the Prof. Responsibility Chapter

What does "contribute to the project management knowledge base" mean?

- Share lessons learned

- Write articles

- Mentor others

- Perform research on best practices

See the Prof. Responsibility Chapter

What does "enhance personal professional competence" mean?

- Understand your own strengths and weaknesses

- Continue to learn

- Look for new practices

See the Prof. Responsibility Chapter

What does "balance
stakeholders' interests"
mean?

Part of "promote interaction among stakeholders", it means:

- Work to get clear and complete project objectives and project requirements

- Understand stakeholders' interests

- Recommend approaches that strive for fair resolution

See the Prof. Responsibility Chapter

What does "interact with team and stakeholders in a professional and cooperative manner" mean?

Part of "promote interaction among stakeholders", it means:

- Respect cultural differences
- Understand others' needs
- Follow practices in other countries, as long as they do not violate laws
- Provide others with project charter, schedule and project management plan they need to do their work

See the Prof. Responsibility Chapter

Notes:

Notes:

Notes:

Notes:

Notes:

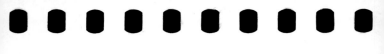

Notes: